IN THE CHICKEN COOP

I0794195

Find and circle the hidden pictures.

apple

comb

crayon

ball

duck

safety cone

lemon

oven mitt

THIS LITTLE PIGGY

Connect the dots from **1** to **20**. Then color the picture.

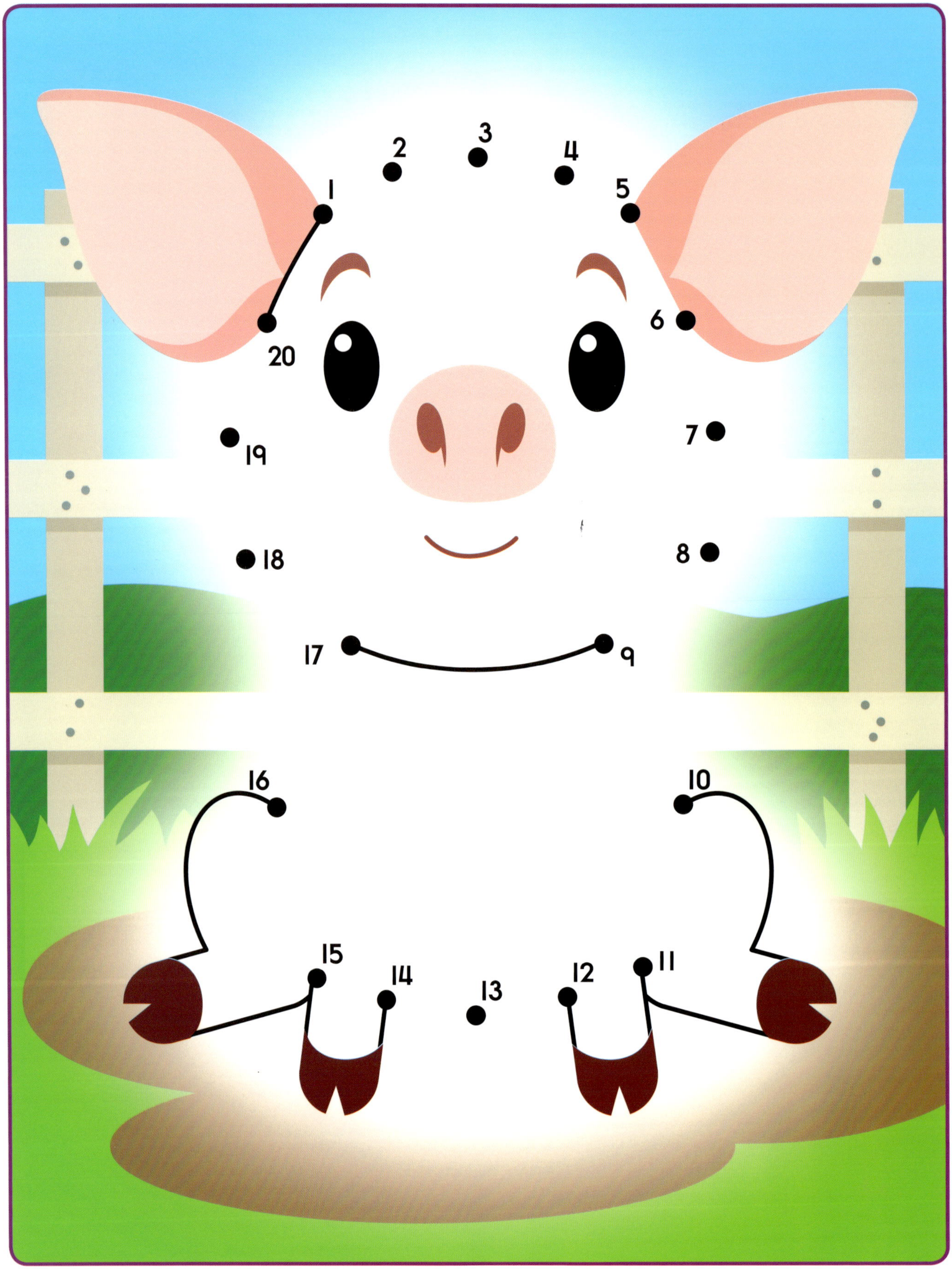

FARMER IN THE FIELD

Finish drawing the picture.

HIDDEN AROUND THE FARM

Find and circle the hidden pictures.

chick | mitten | baseball bat | hippo | ornament | fish | gears | button

tomato
lollipop
moon
spoon
banana
umbrella
sock
pizza slice

HER TOY TRACTOR

Circle **5** things that are different in **picture a** and **picture b**.

SILLY COWS

Circle **8** things that are wrong in the picture.

LOST SHEEP

Help the lamb find its way through the flock of sheep.

Start at the ➡.

A MOMMA AND HER KID

Connect the dots from **1** to **20**. Then color the picture.

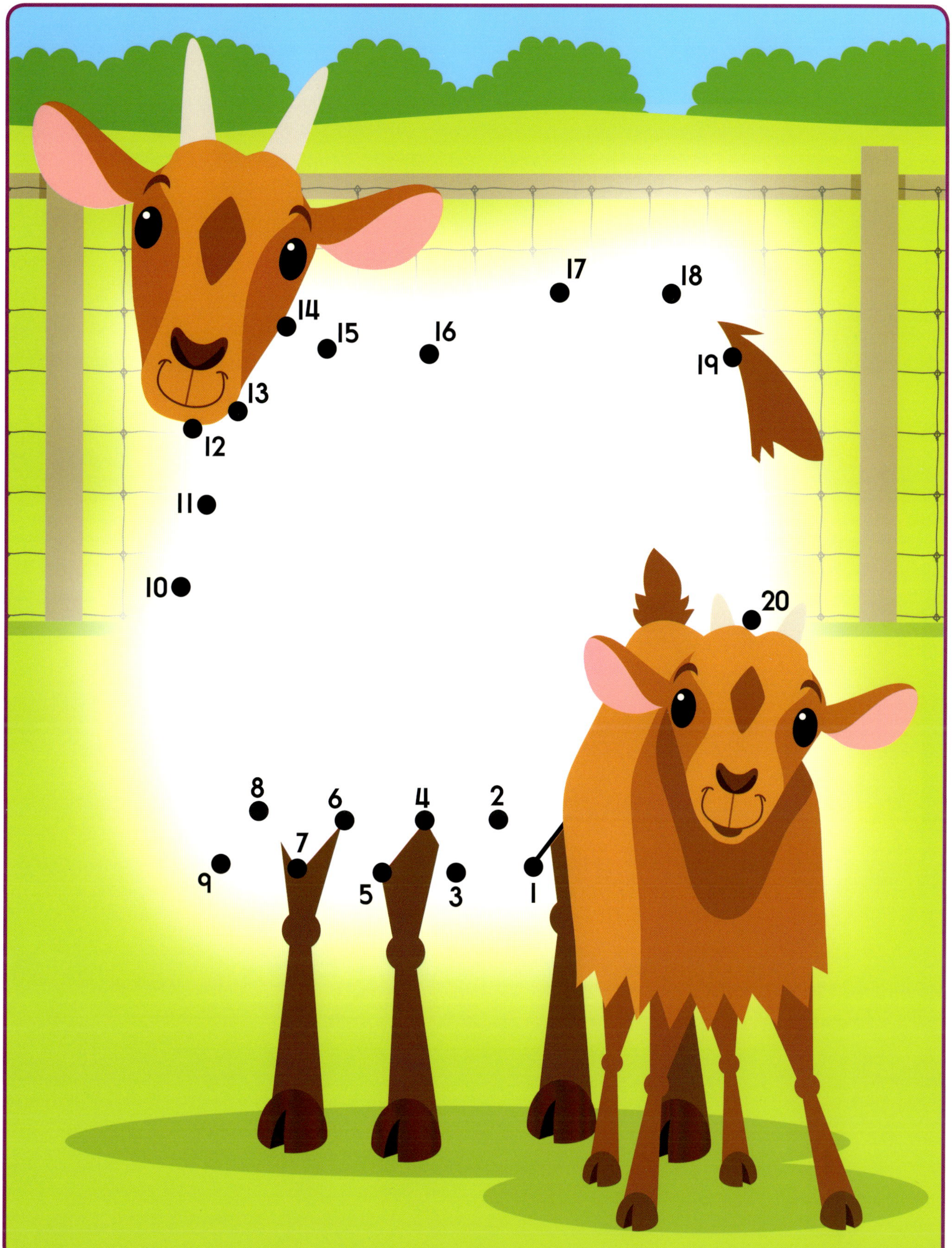

FINDING THINGS IN THE FARMERS MARKET

Find and circle the hidden pictures.

whistle
lightbulb
starfish
grasshopper
seashell
baseball
sandal
football

FARM MARKET

GALLOPING HORSES

Circle **5** things that are different in **picture a** and **picture b**.

PICTURE A

PICTURE B

LOOKING FOR LUNCH

Connect the dots from **1** to **20**. Then color the picture.

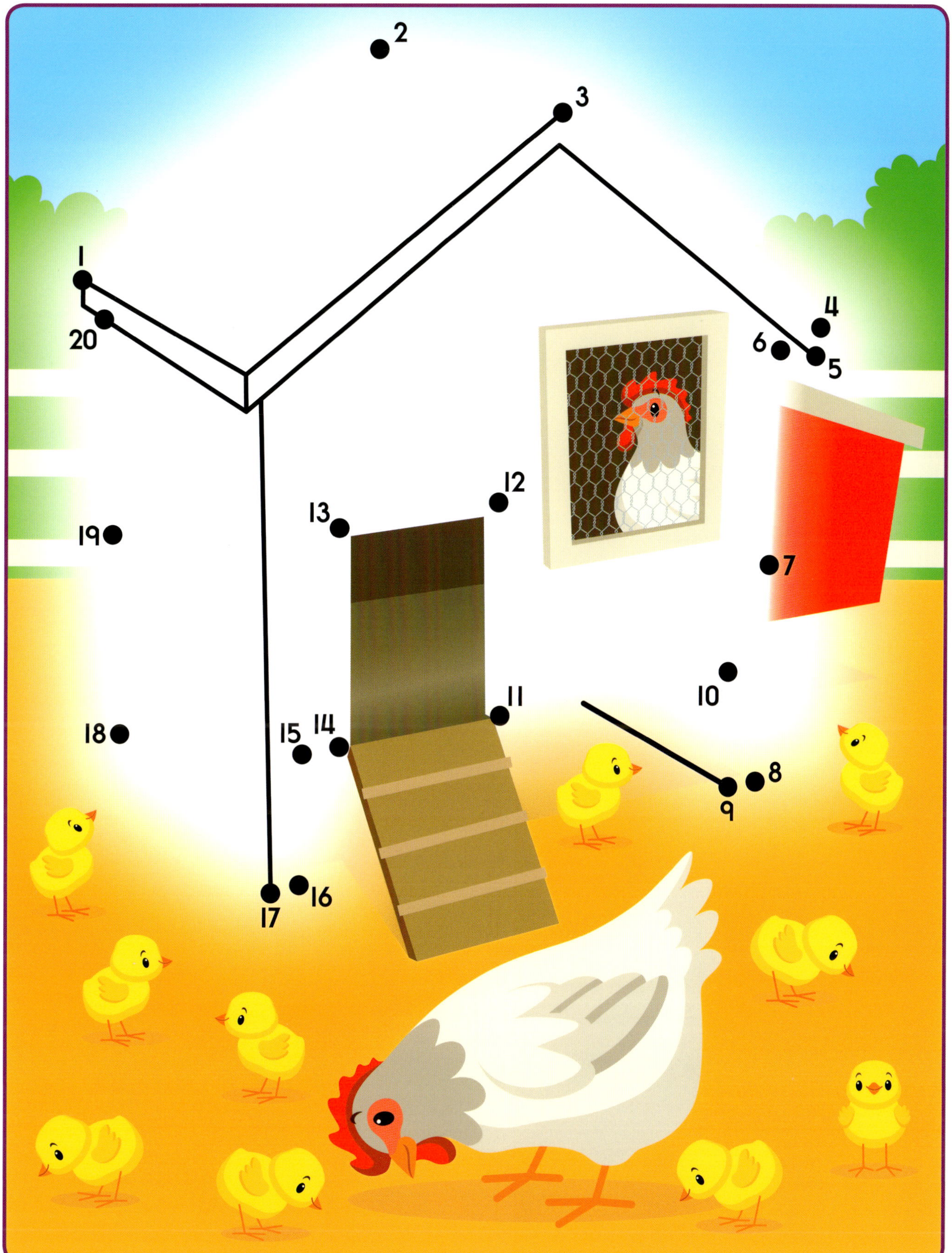

HEAD TO FOOT

Draw a line to connect the animals to their legs.

Start at the ➡.

AROUND THE BARNYARD

Connect the dots from **1** to **20**. Then color the picture.

PORTRAIT OF A PIG

Finish drawing the picture.

LOOKING FOR OUR PARENTS

Help the baby animals find their parents.

Start at the ➡.

PICKING IN THE PUMPKIN PATCH

Connect the dots from **1** to **20**. Then color the picture.

BARN BUDDIES

Find and circle the hidden pictures.

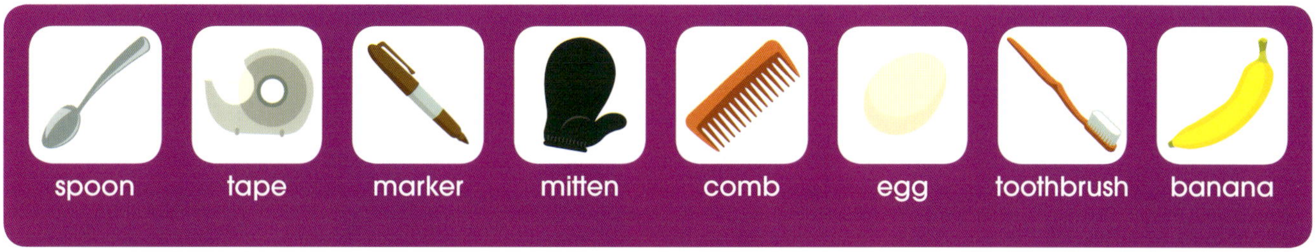

LOOK AT THE LLAMAS

Circle **5** things that are different in **picture a** and **picture b**.

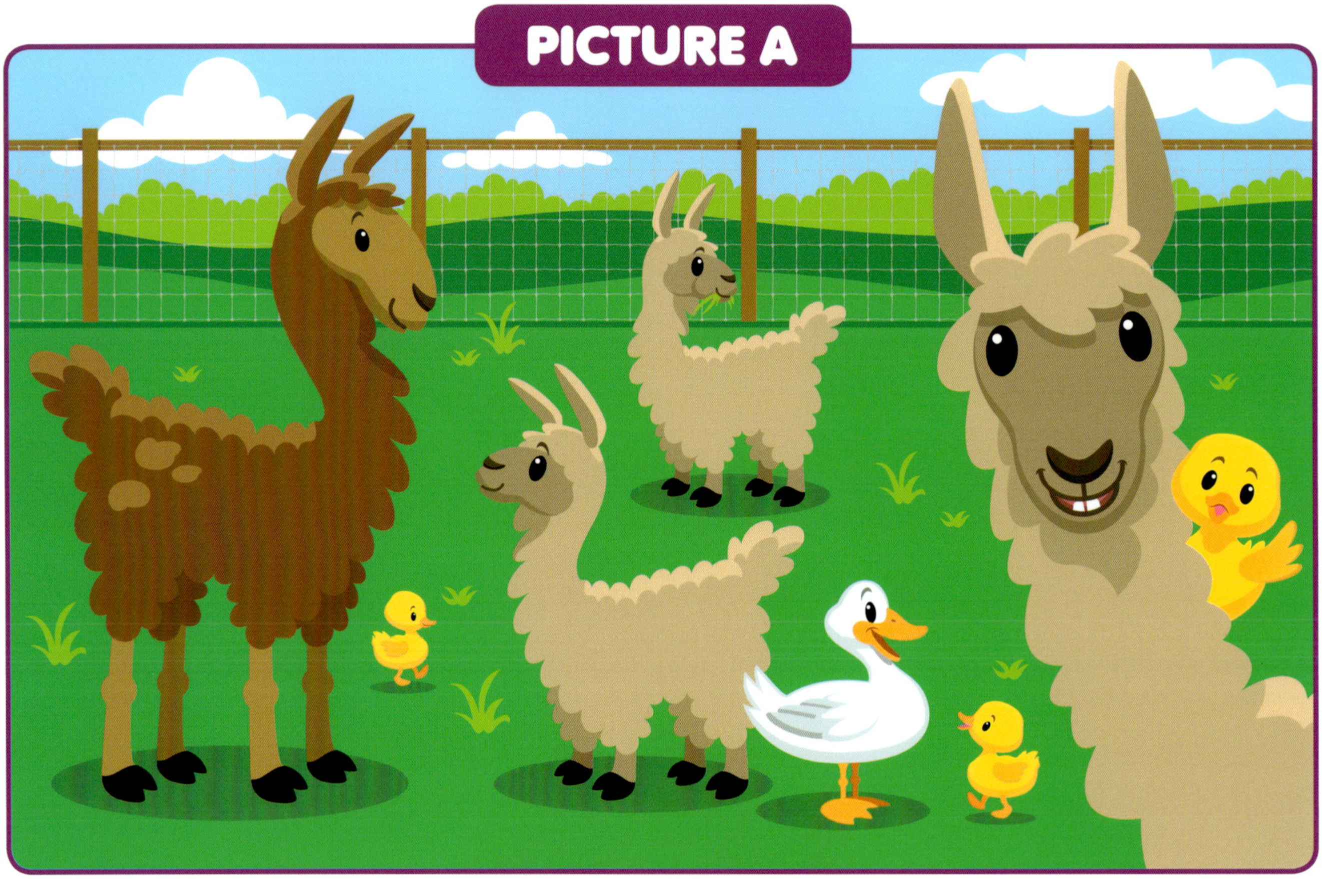

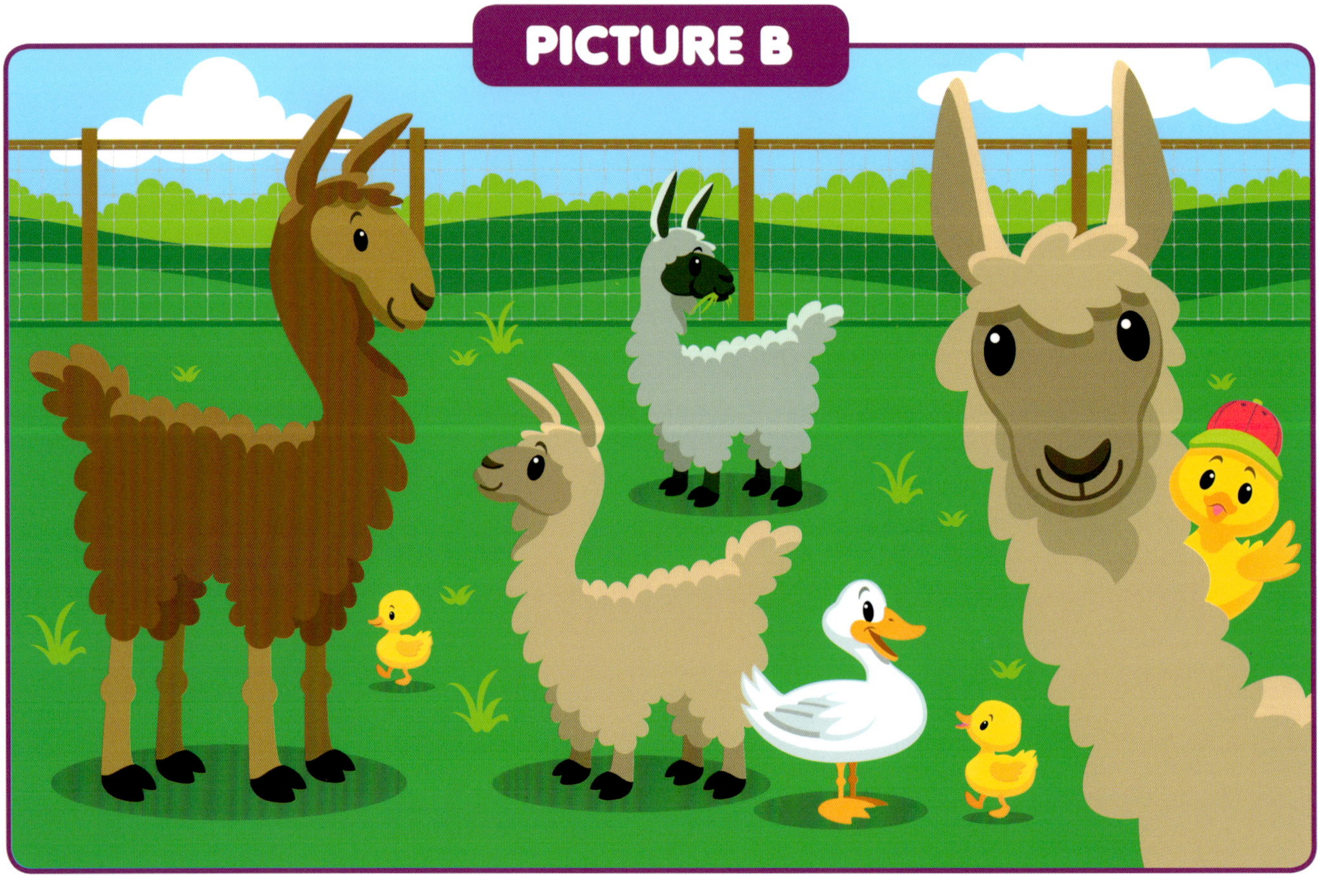

HIKING THROUGH THE HAY BALES

Help the kids find their way to the scarecrow.

Start at the ➡.

DRAWING THE FARMERS' FACES

Draw faces on the farmers.

WORKING IN THE FIELD

Connect the dots from **1** to **20**. Then color the picture.

PORTRAIT OF A CHICKEN

Finish drawing the picture.